W9-AJP-842

Concept and Product Development: Editorial Options, Inc.
Series Designer: Karen Donica
Book Author: Patricia Brennan

For information on other World Book
products, visit us at our Web site at
http://www.worldbook.com

For information on sales to schools and libraries
in the United States, call 1-800-975-3250.

For information on sales to schools and libraries
in Canada, call 1-800-837-5365.

World Book, Inc.
233 N. Michigan Avenue
Chicago, IL 60601

Library of Congress Cataloging-in-Publication Data

Brennan, Patricia.
    Penguins and other flightless birds / [book author, Patricia Brennan].
        p. cm. -- (World Book's animals of the world)
    Summary: Presents information on the physical characteristics, behavior, and natural
    environment of penguins and other flightless birds.
    ISBN 0-7166-1227-5 -- ISBN 0-7166-1223-2 (set)
    1. Penguins--Juvenile literature. 2. Flightless birds--Juvenile literature. [1. Penguins. 2.
Flightless birds.] I. Title. II. Series.

    QL696.S473 B74 2002
    598.47--dc21   2001046710

Printed in Malaysia

1 2 3 4 5 6 7 8 9 06 05 04 03 02

Picture Acknowledgments: Front Cover: © Johnny Johnson, Bruce Coleman Collection; © Jen and Des Bartlett, Bruce Coleman
Inc.; © Robert Maier, Animals Animals; Photo Researchers; © John Shaw, Bruce Coleman Inc.; Jeff Foot, Bruce Coleman Inc.

© Jen and Des Bartlett, Bruce Coleman Inc. 3, 39, 47; © Erwin & Peggy Bauer, Bruce Coleman Inc. 41, 53; © Tim Davis, Photo
Researchers 5, 33, 43, 45; © Tui DeRoy, Bruce Coleman Inc. 31; © Gregory G. Dimijian, Photo Researchers 27; © Jeff Foott,
Bruce Coleman Inc. 59; © George Holton, Photo Researchers 61; © Johnny Johnson, Bruce Coleman Collection 35; © Mark
Jones, Bruce Coleman Inc. 17; © David Madison, Bruce Coleman Inc. 25; © Robert Maier, Animals Animals 57; © Joe
McDonald, Bruce Coleman Inc. 7, 23; © Joe McDonald, Tom Stack & Associates 29; © Tom McHugh, Photo Researchers 51;
© M. Timothy O'Keefe, Bruce Coleman Inc. 4, 21; © Hans Reinhard, Bruce Coleman Inc. 5, 15; © John Shaw, Bruce Coleman
Inc. 19; © Sullivan & Rogers, Bruce Coleman Inc. 49; © Dave Watts, Tom Stack & Associates 13; © Norbert Wu 37; © Gunter
Ziesler, Bruce Coleman Collection, 55.

Illustrations: WORLD BOOK illustration by Michael DiGiorgio 11; WORLD BOOK illustration by Kersti Mack 9, 62.

World Book's Animals of the World

Penguins
and Other Flightless Birds

What makes me a jumping jack?

World Book, Inc.
A Scott Fetzer Company
Chicago

Contents

How do I keep m feathers from being ruffled?

Who needs a sled?

What's all the chatter about?

What Is a Flightless Bird?

As you might guess, a flightless bird is a bird that can't fly. A penguin is a flightless bird. So is the ostrich. Other flightless birds include rheas *(REE uhz),* cassowaries *(KAS uh WEHR eez),* kiwis *(KEE weez)*, and the emu *(EE myoo)*.

All birds have wings. But a flightless bird's wings are usually small for its body. Flapping small wings doesn't provide the "lift" needed to fly. Scientists believe that flightless birds used to be able to fly long ago, when their bodies were smaller. But over time, their bodies became larger even though their wings stayed the same size.

Not all flightless birds are closely related. But they do have much in common with each other and with other birds. All birds are vertebrates *(VUR tuh brihtz),* or animals with backbones. Birds are warm-blooded and hatch from eggs. All birds have feathers, and they have beaks instead of teeth.

Penguin

Where in the World Do Flightless Birds Live?

Most flightless birds live in parts of the Southern Hemisphere. Emus are found in Australia. Rheas live in South America. Ostriches live in Africa—in both the Southern Hemisphere and the Northern Hemisphere. Some kinds of flightless birds live on open plains or in deserts. Others make their homes on islands far out at sea. Penguins spend much of their lives in the ocean.

There are 17 species, or kinds, of penguins. Different penguin species live in different places. Emperor penguins, for example, live along the icy coast of Antarctica. King penguins live along the rocky coastlines of South America and islands just north of Antarctica. Yellow-eyed penguins live off the coast of New Zealand, which is southeast of Australia. Galapagos *(guh LAH puh GOHS)* penguins live farther north than all other penguins. They live along the shores of the Galapagos Islands, west of South America.

World Map

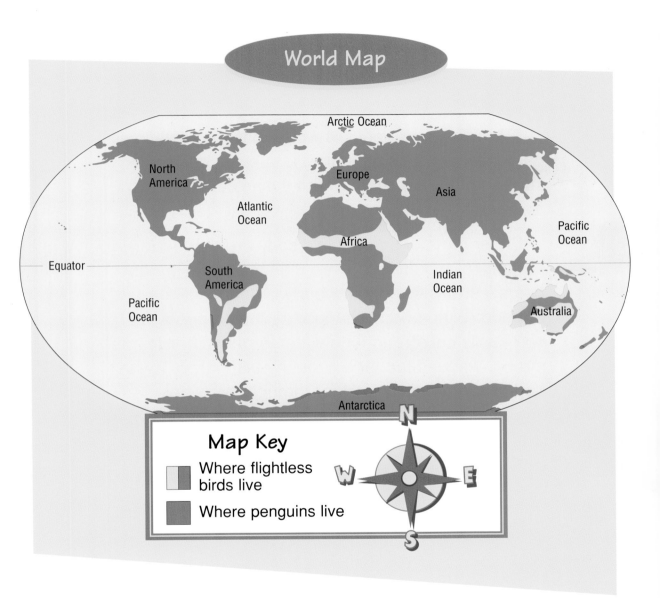

Arctic Ocean

North America

Europe

Asia

Atlantic Ocean

Africa

Pacific Ocean

Equator

South America

Indian Ocean

Pacific Ocean

Australia

Antarctica

Map Key

Where flightless birds live

Where penguins live

N W E S

What Are Penguin Wings Good For?

Penguins have very stiff wings that are sometimes called flippers. Like other flightless birds, penguins can't use their wings to fly. But they can use them to swim.

Other parts of a penguin's body are made for swimming, too. In fact, even the shape of a penguin helps it swim. A penguin's body is shaped like a torpedo. With a body shaped like that, a penguin can easily cut through the water. A penguin also has strong, webbed feet and a stubby tail. It uses its feet and tail as a rudder to steer through the water.

As swimmers, penguins are strong and fast. They usually swim at about 8 miles (13 kilometers) per hour. At this speed, they can travel great distances. In short bursts, they can reach three times that speed.

Penguin Swimming

Tail

Feet

Flippers

11

Can Penguins Breathe Underwater?

No, they cannot. Penguins don't have gills for breathing underwater as fish do. Instead, penguins have lungs—just as people do. That means that they must come to the surface to breathe air.

When penguins need to breathe, they often leap clear out of the water. If they are traveling long distances, they might leap up about once a minute. But if they are fleeing from an enemy such as a leopard seal, some penguins leap clear out of the water every few feet. Besides allowing them to breathe, leaping helps penguins keep away from their enemies down below.

Being able to leap also comes in handy when a penguin needs to get onto ice or land. Most penguins can't pull themselves out of the water onto an icy ledge or a rocky shore with just their flippers. So they leap instead.

Penguins leaping
out of water

How Do Penguins Move About on Land?

Penguins have a few ways of moving about on land. One way is walking—or waddling! Penguins have bodies that are ideal for swimming, but not for walking. Penguins have tall bodies and short legs. This odd combination makes them rock from side to side when they walk. Penguins usually waddle slowly. But when penguins are in a hurry, they can waddle for short distances as fast as a running human.

Some penguins, such as rockhoppers, are good climbers, too. Often, the slopes they climb are icy and steep. But penguins can get a good grip because they have hooked toes. Sometimes penguins even use their bills to get better holds on the rock or ice.

Tobogganing, or sledding, is another way that some penguins move about on land. The emperor penguins you see here are tobogganing over ice and snow on their bellies. They "row" with their flippers and push with their feet.

14

Emperor penguins
tobogganing

What Do Penguins Eat?

Penguins find all their food in the sea. They eat mostly fish and squid, which they catch in their sharp beaks. They also eat crustaceans *(kruhs TAY shuhnz)*, such as crabs, shrimp, and krill.

When a penguin is at sea, it usually eats as much as it can. A large penguin can collect up to 30 fish in one dive. That's a big dinner!

Since they don't have teeth, penguins use their beaks to grab and hold wriggling prey. Spines on the roof of a penguin's beak help this bird get a good grip on its slippery food. Penguins even have spines on their tongues.

Penguins swallow pebbles and stones as well as their regular food. Why? Even scientists aren't sure of the main reason. The stones may help penguins grind up and digest their food. And the stones may add enough extra weight to help penguins when they want to dive down deep.

Penguin searching for prey

Why Do Penguins Swim Together?

Penguins spend some of their time on land or on huge slabs of ice. But when they need to eat, they must return to the water. Most kinds of penguins, like these Adelie *(AD uh lee)* penguins, return to the water in groups. That's because an enemy, such as a leopard seal, may be hiding below the water's surface. A group has more eyes to look out for an oncoming predator. And a nearby predator may have a hard time choosing which penguin to chase. A lone penguin is a much easier target.

Penguins have other enemies in the water to worry about besides leopard seals. Sea lions, sharks, and killer whales all prey on penguins.

On land, adult penguins are usually safe. But chicks that are weak, sickly, or left alone are always at risk of being attacked. Large birds of prey, gulls, and giant petrels eat penguin chicks if given the chance.

Adelie penguins diving

How Do Penguins Stay Warm and Dry?

On top of their skin, penguins have thick coats of feathers. Penguin feathers are good at trapping heat. They are the main reason some penguins can live in such cold places. The feathers are also waterproof. They keep penguins dry underneath, even while the birds are swimming.

If penguins don't keep their feathers in very good shape, they don't stay waterproof. So penguins spend several hours a day preening, or caring for their feathers. Penguins use their beaks, flippers, and feet to preen. For extra protection in the water, penguins spread oil on their feathers. The oil comes from a special gland near their tail feathers.

Penguins that live in cold regions have an extra layer of fat, called *blubber*. The extra layer of fat acts like a blanket to help keep the birds warm when the temperature drops. Penguins also use fat to store energy. That comes in handy when they go long periods without food.

King penguin preening

Why Do Penguins Shed Their Feathers?

Penguins shed their feathers because they become worn and damaged. When penguins shed their old feathers and grow new ones, it is called *molting*. Penguins molt once a year.

Penguins always molt on land or on ice. Until they grow new waterproof coats, they can't go back into the water. And the water is where they need to go to find food.

Sometimes penguins might have to go for more than a month without food while they molt. To prepare, penguins eat as much as they can during the weeks leading up to the molt. Eating so much helps them add fat to their bodies. The penguins live off the fat while they grow new feathers.

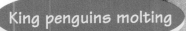
King penguins molting

What Is a Penguin Colony?

Once a year, large groups of penguins return to the land at the same time. They do this to mate and to lay their eggs. Most penguins make their nests in huge gatherings called colonies, such as the one you see here. Notice the large brown penguins at the bottom of the picture. They are adolescent penguins that haven't yet grown their adult black and white feathers. A penguin colony may have thousands of members. In fact, a colony of Adelie or king penguins can have 200,000 pairs of penguins!

Penguins usually form colonies close to where they themselves were born. And it doesn't matter how far away from "home" some penguins are when it's nearly time to mate. Sometimes they return thousands of miles across the open sea to get there.

King penguin colony

How Do Penguins Build Their Nests?

Usually, both male and female penguins work together to build a penguin nest. First, the mates must claim a good spot. In the crowded colonies, this is not easy. Predators are more likely to hunt for eggs and chicks on the edge of a colony. So the good spots are in the center of the nesting grounds.

To make their nests, most penguins dig small holes under large rocks or bushes. Penguins near the South Pole can't dig their nests because the earth is frozen. So they build nests of pebbles on the ground. King and emperor penguins don't build nests at all. They carry their eggs with them on their feet wherever they waddle!

Penguin pair building a nest

What Does It Take to Hatch Penguin Eggs?

Penguin eggs need time and warmth to hatch. Most female penguins lay two eggs. Penguin eggs take 30 days or longer to hatch. The females of larger species, such as king and emperor penguins, lay only one egg. It needs over 60 days to hatch.

Until they hatch, penguin eggs have to stay nearly as warm as an adult penguin's body. Most penguins sit or lie on top of their eggs to keep them warm. This is called *incubation (ihn kyuh BAY shuhn)*. A king or an emperor penguin incubates its lone egg on top of its feet. A special fold of skin covers the egg to keep it warm.

In most species of penguins, both parents take turns looking for food and incubating. But with emperor penguins, the males do all the incubating. Since penguins can't eat while they incubate, male emperors go without food during this period. It may be 65 days before males can return to the sea and eat.

28

Emperor penguin
holding an egg

What Are Penguin Chicks Like?

Baby penguins don't look like their parents—they look more like puffballs! Fuzzy coats of feathers, called *down*, cover the chicks from their heads to their feet. As the chicks grow older, they lose their fluffy feathers. Over time, they grow adult feathers.

Parents must guard their chicks until they are strong enough to protect themselves. Penguin parents pass food they've partly digested to their chicks with their beaks. It's easier for the chicks to swallow food "served" like this.

Some kinds of penguin chicks stay at their nests for just the first two months of their lives. Others stay near the nest up to a year. The parents don't guard them the entire year, but they do feed them. When young penguins are old enough, they leave the colony and learn to feed themselves at sea. Most return to land only to molt and to nest.

Chinstrap penguin
with chicks

Do Penguins Make a Lot of Noise?

Yes! Penguins in a colony can make a lot of noise when they call to one another. Calling is important because parents and chicks can recognize each other by their voices. Without their calls, penguin families could easily lose track of each other in such crowded places.

Nearly every bird species has its own special calls, and so does each kind of penguin. Some penguin calls sound like the cackle of a hen. Some boom like a trumpet. Others even have a harsh cry that sounds like the braying of a donkey!

Penguins communicate in other ways, too. They may wave their heads and flippers. Sometimes they bow. When penguins fight for nesting spots, they may try to stare down one another. They also point at each other with their beaks. If one penguin just isn't getting the message, another penguin may even charge!

Chinstrap penguins calling

Are All Penguins Black and White?

All adult penguins have dark backs and white or yellowish-white fronts. Their dark backs are usually black. However, their beaks, necks, and feet may be brightly colored. Some penguins also have colorful crests of feathers on their heads.

A penguin's coloring comes in very handy. It camouflages *(KAM uh flahzh uhz)* the bird, or helps it blend in with its surroundings. A school of fish swimming above a penguin may not even notice the bird. That's because the penguin's dark back blends in with the dark waters below it. An enemy or prey may not see a penguin swimming above it either. That's because the penguin's pale belly blends with the bright light of the sky or ice above it.

A penguin's dark back may also keep it from getting too cold. Dark colors soak in, or absorb, sunlight. Scientists think penguins may use their backs to get warmer when they float on their stomachs in cold seas.

King penguins

How Do Penguins Dive Really Deep?

Penguins, including the emperor penguins shown here, flap their wings, or flippers, to dive deep. Most other diving birds use their feet to push themselves through water. Birds that dive using their feet don't usually go as deep as penguins do using their flippers.

An emperor penguin can dive deeper than any other bird. It can go down as deep as 1,750 feet (530 meters)! That's deeper than the height of the tallest building in the world! When diving, an emperor penguin can hold its breath for nearly 20 minutes.

This superb diver is also the largest of all penguin species. An adult emperor can be just over 4 feet (1.2 meters) tall and weigh around 85 pounds (38 kilograms).

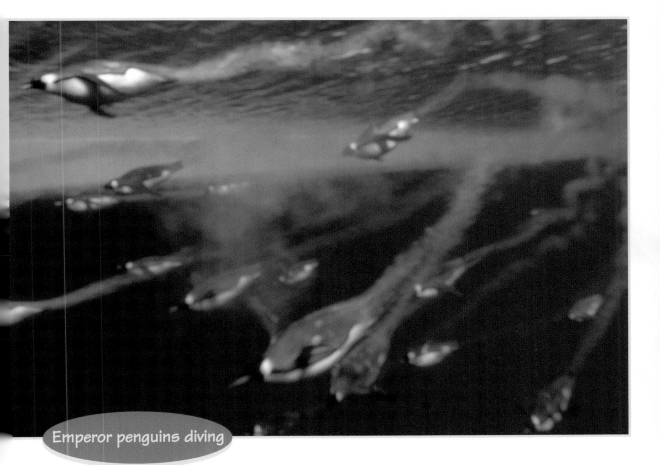

Emperor penguins diving

How Did Rockhoppers Get Their Name?

Rockhoppers got their name because of the way they hop up steep, rocky slopes. These penguins hop up the slopes with both their feet together. Many rockhoppers live in the rocky Falkland Islands, off the southern coast of South America. People there call them "jumping jacks."

Rockhoppers need to hop because they nest up to 500 feet (150 meters) above the sea. Having nests up high keeps rockhoppers safe from leopard seals, which often hunt these birds near the shore. Luckily for rockhoppers, leopard seals aren't good climbers!

As you can see, a rockhopper's head is very colorful. This bird has a bright orange-red bill, a yellow crest, and red eyes. A rockhopper weighs about 6 pounds (3 kilograms) and stands about 22 inches (56 centimeters) tall.

Rockhopper penguin

How Small Is the Smallest Penguin?

The penguin pictured here is called the little penguin. It got its name because it's the smallest penguin of all. It stands only about 16 inches (40 centimeters) tall and weighs about 2 pounds (1 kilogram). The little penguin is more than three times smaller than the emperor penguin.

Little penguins live in dunes on the shores of Australia and New Zealand. They stay in burrows along the coast. They can build their own burrows, but they also use natural cracks in rocks or old nests left by other birds. Each day they leave their burrows behind to hunt for food at sea. At dusk, they return to land and crawl back into their burrows.

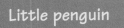
Little penguin

Just What Are Ratites?

Ratites *(RAT yts)* are a large group of flightless birds. This group includes the ostrich, the emu, rheas, cassowaries, and kiwis. Like penguins, ratites are flightless. However, they are not closely related to penguins.

Like penguins and other birds, ratites have feathers. Most kinds of ratites are bigger than most kinds of penguins. And while penguins are great swimmers, no ratites can swim. Instead, ratites get around by walking and running. In fact, the ostrich can run faster than any other kind of bird.

Ostriches

Which Flightless Bird Is the Biggest?

The ostrich is the biggest of all the flightless birds. It's also the biggest bird alive today. An ostrich stands nearly 8 feet (2.4 meters) tall and weighs up to 345 pounds (156 kilograms). Even an ostrich egg is big—about 20 inches (51 centimeters) around. Just one ostrich egg weighs about 3 pounds (1.4 kilograms). That's about the weight of 25 chicken eggs!

Not only do these big birds stand above all other birds, but they also stand out because of their striking looks. A female ostrich has dull brown feathers, but a male has a thick, black-and-white coat. The long, fluffy, white feathers on a male's wings and tail are called plumes.

Ostriches have bald heads. The bare skin of ostriches can be pink or blue. Their eyes are big and round. And their eyelashes are long and thick.

Ostrich

How Fast Can an Ostrich Run?

An ostrich can run very fast! In fact, it's one of the fastest runners on Earth. This bird can reach speeds up to 40 miles (65 kilometers) an hour. Its legs reach out in huge strides. A single stride may be over 15 feet (4.6 meters) long! An ostrich can even outrun a four-legged predator such as a lion.

An ostrich can run fast because of its long legs. Its feet are also well shaped for moving quickly across the ground. The ostrich is the only bird that has just two toes on each foot. This bird's feet are shaped to support the ostrich's heavy weight. They also give the bird solid footing when it pushes off with its powerful legs.

Ostriches on the run do not tire easily. They can run at top speed for about 20 minutes. But ostriches usually run only when they are threatened.

Ostrich running

Do Ostriches Live in Flocks?

Ostriches spend much of their time alone, but they are never too far from members of their family group. A family group is made up of one male and three to five adult females. Sometimes, many ostriches join together to form a flock. A flock of ostriches may contain 50 birds or more. Ostriches usually form flocks in areas that have plenty of food or that are near water holes.

Wild ostriches can be found only in Africa. There, they live on open plains where they can find plenty of their favorite foods: grass and small plants. They also eat bugs and small reptiles, such as turtles and lizards.

A flock of ostriches

Does an Ostrich Hide Its Head in the Sand?

From a distance, it may look as if this is what an ostrich sometimes does. But the ostrich is not hiding. It is just moving eggs around in its nest. Of course, it has to poke its bill into the sand to do that.

A male ostrich builds the nest. He digs a shallow hole in the sand. He then uses the nest to attract mates. Usually, three to five females lay their eggs in the nest. After two or three weeks, the nest contains 30 eggs or more. But many of the eggs are pushed aside so that only about 20 are incubated.

Who incubates the eggs? The male and usually the oldest female in the family group take turns. After about six weeks, the eggs are ready to hatch. When an ostrich chick hatches, it's not much taller than the egg it was curled up in. After a month, it is about the size of an adult chicken. By that time, it can run as fast as an adult ostrich.

Ostrich moving
its eggs

Are There Ostriches in South America?

No, but flightless birds called rheas live in South America. Although rheas and ostriches live thousands of miles apart, they look a lot alike. In fact, they look so much alike that rheas are often called South American ostriches.

Still, there are some differences in their looks. Rheas are smaller than ostriches. The largest kind of rhea stands about 5 feet (1.5 meters) tall and weighs about 50 pounds (23 kilograms). Rheas have three toes on each foot, while ostriches have only two. Rheas have feathers on their necks and heads, but ostriches do not.

Rheas live in flocks of 5 to 30 birds on open grasslands. Rheas feed on leaves, roots, and insects.

Rhea

What Big Bird Has Very Tiny Wings?

The emu is a large flightless bird with feathers that look like shaggy fur. An emu grows 5 to 6 feet (1.5 to 1.8 meters) tall and may weigh over 100 pounds (45 kilograms). That's big enough to make it the second-largest flightless bird. However, its wings are only about 7 inches (18 centimeters) long. That's shorter than a crow's wings! An emu's wings are so small that the bird's thick coat of feathers covers them over.

Emus are found only in Australia. There, they travel in pairs or small groups on the grassy plains. They eat fruit, seeds, and bugs. As they search for food, they sometimes anger farmers by eating crops.

Like the ostrich, the emu is a speedy animal. An emu can run nearly 30 miles (50 kilometers) per hour, taking 9-foot (2.7-meter) strides. This can help an emu escape danger.

Emus

Where Do Cassowaries Live?

Cassowaries live in dense forests in New Guinea *(GIHN ee)* and Australia. These birds have large, bony growths on their bright blue heads. The growth is called a *casque (KASK).* Cassowaries use their casques to butt through the thick forest undergrowth.

A cassowary can grow nearly 5 feet (1.5 meters) tall and weigh about 120 pounds (54 kilograms). In spite of its big size, a cassowary is a shy creature. It moves about the forest only at night, feeding on fruits and small animals. When it's in danger, a cassowary attacks with its feet. Each foot has a long claw that is sharp enough to kill an enemy.

Cassowary

What Are the Smallest Ratites?

Kiwis are the smallest ratites by far. The largest kind of kiwi is only 22 inches (56 centimeters) in length, not including its long beak. Kiwis have no tails, and their feathers look like hair. Their beaks are long, thin, and flexible. Perhaps oddest of all, their nostrils are located at the tips of their bills—not the tops.

People rarely see kiwis in the wild. That's because kiwis sleep during the day in burrows and come out only at night. When feeding, they poke their beaks into the ground in search of their favorite foods—worms and other invertebrates, or animals without backbones. Having nostrils at the ends of their beaks helps kiwis smell where these animals are hiding.

Kiwi

Are Flightless Birds in Danger?

Some flightless birds are in danger. The ostrich can no longer be found in much of its original habitat. The Galapagos penguin is in danger of becoming extinct, or dying out completely.

Flightless birds are in danger for many reasons. People have turned the feeding grounds of rheas and the ostrich into grazing lands for farms. People also hunt many flightless birds for their feathers, meat, and skin.

Oil spills from ships are a serious danger to penguins. Even a small amount of oil of this kind can hurt a penguin's feathers and destroy its ability to stay warm in cold seas. Overfishing is also harmful to penguins. When too many fish are taken from the seas, these birds can lose much of the food they depend on.

International laws have been passed to protect many flightless birds. In addition, some of these wild animals are bred on farms.

Galapagos penguin

Flightless Bird Fun Facts

- → Ever since ancient times, people have used ostrich eggshells as drinking cups and containers.

- → A female kiwi lays just one egg, but it's a big one. Her egg weighs one-fourth of her own body weight!

- → An ostrich can run twice as fast as a swallow can fly.

- → Some penguins can travel 75 miles (120 kilometers) over the frozen sea—mostly by tobogganing.

- → Little penguins are also known as fairy penguins.

- → An ostrich can live to be 70 years old.

Glossary

bill A bird's beak.

blubber Thick fat under the skin of some penguins that keeps them warm and stores energy.

camouflage To help blend in with the surroundings.

casque A large, bony growth on the head of a cassowary.

chick A young penguin.

colony A large group of nesting penguins.

crustacean A group of animals with hard shells that live mostly in water.

down Soft, puffy feathers.

flipper A penguin's wing.

flock A large group of birds that stay together.

gill The breathing organ of animals that live in water.

hatch To bring forth young from an egg.

incubation Keeping eggs warm enough so that they will hatch.

invertebrate An animal without a backbone.

molt To shed feathers and grow new ones in their place.

predator An animal that lives by hunting and killing other animals for food.

preen To care for coat of feathers or fur.

prey Any animal that is hunted for food by another animal.

ratite A group of related species of flightless birds.

toboggan To sled.

vertebrate An animal with a backbone.

waddle To walk with short steps and a swaying motion.

waterproof To not let water through.

Index

(**Boldface** indicates a photo, map, or illustration.)

For more information about flightless birds, try these resources:

Ostriches, Emus, Rheas, Kiwis and Cassowaries, by Ann Elwood and John Bonnet Wexo, Creative Education, 2000.

Penguins, by Wayne Lynch, Firefly Books, 1999.

A Visual Introduction to Penguins, by Bernhard Stonehouse, Checkmark Books, 1999.

http://www.enchantedlearning.com/subjects/birds/printouts/Flightless.shtml

http://www.pbs.org/wnet/nature/penguins/index.html

http://www.terraquest.com/va/science/penguins/penguins.html

Flightless Bird Classification

Scientists classify animals by placing them into groups. The animal kingdom is a group that contains all the world's animals. Phylum, class, order, and family are smaller groups. Each phylum contains many classes. A class contains orders, an order contains families, and a family contains individual species. Each species also has its own scientific name. Here is how the animals in this book fit in to this system.

Animals with backbones and their relatives (Phylum Chordata)

Birds (Class Aves)

Penguins and their relatives (Order Ciconiiformes)

Penguins (Family Spheniscidae)

Adelie penguin . . . . *Pygoscelis adeliae*

Chinstrap penguin . . . . *Pygoscelis antarctica*

Emperor penguin . . . . *Aptenodytes forsteri*

Galapagos penguin . . . . *Spheniscus mendiculus*

King penguin . . . . *Aptenodytes patagonicus*

Little (fairy) penguin . . . . *Eudyptula minor*

Rockhopper penguin . . . . *Eudyptes chrysocome*

Yellow-eyed penguin . . . . *Megadyptes antipodes*

Ratites (Order Struthioniformes)

Cassowaries (Family Casuariidae)

Emu (Family Dromaiidae)

Emu . . . . *Dromaius novaehollandiae*

Kiwis (Family Apterygidae)

Ostrich (Family Struthionidae)

Ostrich . . . . *Struthio camelus*

Rheas (Family Rheidae)